VINTAGE & HISTORIC
DRAG RACERS

Robert Genat

MBI Publishing Company

First published in 1998 by MBI Publishing Company, 729 Prospect Avenue, PO Box 1, Osceola, WI 54020-0001 USA.

MBI Publishing Company books are also available at discounts in bulk quantity for industrial or sales-promotional use. For details write to Special Sales Manager at Motorbooks International Wholesalers & Distributors, 729 Prospect Avenue, PO Box 1, Osceola, WI 54020-0001 USA.

Library of Congress Cataloging-in-Publication Data

Genat, Robert.
　　　Vintage & historic drag racers/ Robert Genat.
　　　　　p.　cm. -- (Enthusiast color series)
　　　Includes index.
　　　ISBN 0-7603-0435-1 (paperback : alk. paper)
　　　1. Dragsters--History. 2. Antique and Classic
　　　cars. I. Title. II. Series.
　　　TL236.2.G46 1998　　　　　　98-3916
　　　629.228--dc21

On the front cover: With all eight candles lit, the Kent Fuller Magicar Top Fuel dragster appears ready to race. High fashion for any dragster driver in the mid-sixties was the aluminized driver's suit and face mask. Though crude, these early fire suits saved many front-engine dragster drivers from apocalyptic fires resulting from an engine explosion. *Robert Genat*

On the frontis: When drag racing began, there were no big sponsors or heavily funded points championships to win at the end of the year. Drag racing was done for the thrill of competition and a simple trophy. *Robert Genat*

On the title page: The Albertson Olds dragster, Top Eliminator at the 1960 NHRA Nationals, rests peacefully on the Pomona Drag Strip, site of the first drag race sanctioned by the NHRA. *Robert Genat*

On the back cover: Tony Nancy's good friend, Tom Sparks, leans over to give him a few last minute instructions prior to making a run down the San Fernando Raceway. The light blue 1951 Ford Woody wagon behind the roadster is Nancy's shop car (note lettering on the door). Several changes were made to the car by the time it appeared in *Hot Rod* magazine's December, 1957, issue. *Dan LaCroix collection*

Edited by: Ann Mckenna
Designed by: Katie L. Sonmor

Printed in Hong Kong through World Print, Ltd.

DEDICATION

To my dear Aunt Wilma Potochan, a lady with a heart of gold and the courage of any drag racer in this book. Her one and only drag race was 40 years ago on the streets of Southern California. A car full of kids had been taunting her at every stoplight along Ventura Boulevard. Finally, she'd had enough and floored the accelerator on her brand-new 1957 Pontiac. When she reached 80 miles an hour, the young whippersnappers were nowhere to be seen.

CONTENTS

ACKNOWLEDGMENTS

The list of participants in this book is long and illustrious. At the top of that list has to be Wally Parks. He founded the NHRA (National Hot Rod Association) and took this new form of racing off the streets and gave it a safe home. His foresight and guidance have given us the most spectacular and fastest side-by-side form of motor sport in the world. In addition to that, he is a truly nice guy.

Greg Sharp has the enviable task of guarding the Holy Grail of the NHRA archives. He also coordinates the NHRA's annual Hot Rod Reunion. During the research phase of this project, he was putting the finishing touches on the new NHRA Museum. Time was a very precious resource to Greg, but he gave me an abundance of it for my project. His and the NHRA's cooperation were very important to the success of this book. Thanks, Greg!

"Big Daddy" Don Garlits is a living legend. Those words don't seem adequate to describe a man who's a national treasure in the eyes of anyone who loves drag racing. I stand in awe of his accomplishments. I also stand in awe of him as a gentleman. It was an honor and privilege to spend two days at his Ocala, Florida, Museum of Drag Racing, photographing cars and reminiscing with Big Daddy. Thanks, Big! A special thanks to Greg Capitano, the Museum's general manager, and his staff, for moving the cars I wanted to photograph through the tight confines within the museum.

Thanks to the following drag racing legends for reminiscing with me about their early days in the sport: Don Prudhomme, Mike Kuhl, Gene Mooneyham, "Jungle Larry" Faust, Jeep Hampshire, Charlie Di Bari, Tony Nancy, and Kent Fuller. It was a thrill talking to you guys.

Thanks to car owners Chuck Einolander and Ralph Candee (Einolander and Candee dragster) Garry Newton (Larson Ford A/FX 1965 Mustang); Dan and Robin LaCroix (Tony Nancy's 22Jr. Roadster); Bob Mosher (1963 *Melrose Missile III*); Jerry Bryant (1963 Z-11 Chevy); Mickey Weise (1968 Hemi Dart); and Tom and Linda Jacobson (1962 409 Chevy). Thanks for preserving these historical gems. A special thanks to Bill Pitts, owner of the *Magicar* Top Fuel dragster, for "tipping the can" so his beautiful dragster would light the night sky—making our ears ring and our eyes water.

Thanks to the following folks who found data, pushed cars, polished mag wheels, held reflectors, and shined chrome. The following were the best team of researchers and photo assistants money couldn't buy: Al Lugo, Bill Larzelere, Bill Corbett, Joel Naprstek, Dr. Marvin Smith, Aimee LaCroix, Mike LaCroix, Bob LaBonté, Tom Morris, Linda Morris, Dave Wear Jr., John Weiderler, Mark Farrin, Kris Farrin, Steve Froland, Steve Powers, Jim Hoy, Rick McDonald, Vince Yamasaki, Mike Hassett, Bob Bland, and Marvin Wait. A special thanks to my good friend, Joe Veraldi, who in addition to helping during photo shoots, took me on "Mr. Toad's Wild Ride" in the Mooneyham coupe when we towed it out of Garlits' Museum.

—*Robert Genat*

INTRODUCTION

On a warm summer night in July 1959, I was sitting at my workbench in the basement of my parents' suburban Detroit home, working on an AMT model car. The AM radio on the shelf was tuned to WXYZ, the hottest rock and roll radio station in Detroit. Disc jockey Tom Clay had just finished playing Wilbert Harrison's *Kansas City*, and he was doing an ad for a local television store, which I mentally tuned out. Suddenly, I was jolted by those three famous words *"SUNDAY!—SUNDAY!—SUNDAY!"* The excited announcer went on to describe the upcoming match race at Detroit Dragway as though it were the Christians versus the lions. I had to go.

I bugged my older brother until he relented to let me tag along. The first trip to a drag strip was a big event for a boy of 13. Back then, I spent every dime of my allowance on hot rod magazines and model cars—I was car-crazy. I'll never forget the sight of seeing a dragster run for the first time. It was Setto Postoian. He took his dragster down Detroit Dragway at a top speed of 163 miles per hour and his elapsed time was somewhere in the mid-nine-second range. Not very impressive by today's standards, but out of this world for a 13-year-old kid in 1959.

I was captivated by the variety of hot rods, dragsters, gassers, and stock cars that were racing. Every car I read about on the pages of those magazines came to life in front of me on that quarter-mile of asphalt. The smell of burning rubber and the cackle of open exhaust headers were like a narcotic—I was hooked for life. I was even overwhelmed by the variety of custom cars and hot rods I saw in the spectator parking lot. Whenever I could convince my brother to take me to the strip, we went.

On Labor Day weekend in 1960, I was lucky enough to attend the NHRA U.S. National Championship Drags at Detroit Dragway. We staked out a spot along the return road fence at midtrack. It was there that I saw Leonard Harris take Top Eliminator in the Albertson Olds dragster, a car I would photograph (and sit in) for this book, 37 years later. At the Nationals that year, *Motor Trend* magazine awarded the trophy for the Best Engineered car to Dode Martin and Jim Nelson for the Dragmaster *Two Thing*. Little did I know that 32 years later, Dode Martin, at the Oceanside, California, Dragmaster shop, would be reworking a driveshaft for my 1962 Chevy.

For the next six years I was a regular at Detroit Dragway, whether helping someone who was racing his car, as a spectator, or racing my own car. Today, I still attend the drags as a casual competitor and an avid spectator. It's definitely an addiction that's hard to break.

Since the first time I attended a drag race, the sport has dramatically evolved. Speeds have increased, but the format has stayed the same—quarter-mile from a standing start, first one to the end is the winner. Since its inception, organized drag racing has been a sport in which anyone can participate. It's the simplest form of racing with a class for almost any type of vehicle. Drag racing is also the fastest side-by-side automotive racing in the world.

Drag racing was born on the streets of Southern California with hot rods that ran on the dry lakes fueling the fire. Those dry lake meets were held monthly and were quite a distance from the boulevards of Los Angeles. Many hot rodders used the streets to test their cars against a friend's car in casual competition.

Wally Parks, who later formed the National Hot Rod Association (NHRA) reminisces, "My first memory of drag racing goes back to the pre-World War II years, when this was a popular after-hours activity on streets and outlying areas in and around Los Angeles. I can very definitely recall the first one of these I attended, which was out on Westminster Boulevard, where the Los Angeles International Airport is today. It was simply a matter of people going out there at night when there was very little traffic. The onlookers lined up alongside the road. This happened to be a divided highway and the individuals who were racing simply paired off two at a time. At a common consent signal, they would race for whatever distance was predetermined. It would usually be for about a half-mile. Then they would return back to the crowd, enjoying the satisfaction of winning or the humiliation of losing. Then another pair would go. This was the type of street racing that began to take place throughout Southern California and in other areas. It was something that became a public nuisance and a problem for law enforcement agencies."

By the time the war ended, the incidences of street racing were increasing. It was becoming a serious public safety problem.

In 1949, Parks, then editor of *Hot Rod* magazine, ran tests at unused airports to see how far a car could accel-erate and then safely stop. Parks' tests determined that a quarter-mile was that distance. In 1951, Parks formed the NHRA. "Dedicated to Safety" was the motto of this fledgling association. Parks believed that organization was necessary to promote safety, provide structure, and improve the tarnished image of hot rodders. He focused on developing rules and standards for the racing events to be held on these early drag strips. Many of the procedures and classes were borrowed from those that had been developed by the Southern California Timing Association (SCTA) for its dry lakes competition.

On April 12 and 13, 1953, the NHRA held its first officially sanctioned drag race at the new drag strip at the Los Angeles County Fairgrounds in Pomona. Over that weekend, a crowd estimated at between 15,000 and 20,000 people watched 375 cars in competition. In 1954, Pomona Police Chief Ralph Parker assigned motor sergeant, Bud Coons, to work with the NHRA's Safety Safari. Coons traveled across the country for three years setting up and organizing NHRA-sanctioned drag strips. In 1955, the NHRA held its first National Championship Drag Races in Great Bend, Kansas. It was the start of something big.

The drag racing cars of the 1950s were very unsophisticated. Racers had one goal—to go fast. Each had his own theory of how to build a winning car and in the 1950s, everyone built his own car, since kits were not available. Early racers found that the reduction of weight was like raising horsepower. So, they began stripping anything and everything off their cars. Some cars consisted of just an engine in a bare frame with a small seat. These wily competitors also found that by running exotic fuels they could increase their speed. In some cases, this additional speed exceeded the stopping power of the car's brakes.

The 1960s saw an explosion of drag racing across the country. More and more tracks were

Dragster drivers of the 1960s were courageous souls who pushed home-built machines to intense speeds. Sitting inches off the ground, they often had to look around the engine's supercharger just to see where the car was going. This driver is wearing a Racemask, designed by Tony Nancy in 1961 to protect a dragster driver's face from fire and flying debris in case of an engine explosion.

being built and sanctioned specifically for drag racing. In 1961, the NHRA added the Pomona Winter-nationals to their schedule. At that event, a noticeable in-crease in the amount of Super Stock entries was seen. These Super Stock cars of the early 1960s grew into the highly modified factory experimental cars of the mid-1960s. By the end of the decade, these cars barely resembled a production line car in their form as crowd-pleasing Funny Cars. In 1963, the "Christmas Tree" was introduced at the starting line. It replaced the human starter who stood in the middle of the track with a flag in his hand. Also in 1963, the NHRA lifted its fuel ban. In the mid-1960s, the popularity of Top Fuel dragsters was at an all-time high with over 300 Top Fuel rails running. Late in the decade, both M & H and Goodyear had developed better compounds for their slicks. This allowed the dragsters to get the power to the ground and speeds increased.

The 1970s saw the sport of drag racing change from a hobby to a business. No longer could a group of enthusiasts pool their money and talent to build a competitive car. A sponsor was needed to fund the car and all of the things needed to make it competitive. Rear-engine dragsters were the norm and Funny Cars were no longer for special exhibitions or match races, but were a regular competition class. The factory Super Stockers were now in a class called Pro Stock. These cars resembled production cars, but were highly modified. The sides of the dragsters and Funny Cars were larger, allowing increased visibility of the sponsors' names. More national events were added. Speeds increased and elapsed times decreased in all classes.

In this book, I've tried to find a wide range of types and styles of drag racing cars from 1956 through 1975. To the best of my knowledge and research, all of the cars in this book are the real thing: no clone cars, no fakes. Many of the stories are from the brave people who owned and raced the cars depicted in this book.

Did you hear that? The tower has just announced that the first round of eliminations has ended. The second round won't be starting for a little while. Let's grab our pit passes and take a walk through the pits to take a closer look at these vintage and historic drag racers.

CHAPTER 1

MELVIN HEALTH'S *DRAGSTER*

In 1954, the NHRA held its first regional Championship Drag Meet in Caddo Mills, Texas. One of the attendees was a young hot rodder from Rush Springs, Oklahoma, by the name of Melvin Heath. He brought a rather rickety-looking car to that meet and received a lot of criticism for its construction. Heath's car was built on a pair of frail Model T frame rails, and it was powered by a stock Chrysler engine running on pump gas. What Heath's car lacked in workmanship, it made up for in performance. It was the fastest of the gas-burning cars and was finally beaten in the last Top Eliminator race by a dragster burning nitro.

Melvin Heath's 1956 Championship-winning dragster has a slender body with bulges to accommodate the engine. The small opening in the upper portion of the cowling is to allow air flow to the carburetors. Like most dragsters, it has only rear brakes.
INSET

Hot rodders and drag racers were the early adapters of multiple carburetors. The most popular carburetor was the dual-throat Stromberg 97. Melvin Heath mounted six of these atop a Crower U-FAB manifold he had to weld together.

Melvin Heath's dragster had the basic look of a sprint car with the driver sitting aft over the rear axle. The rear tires were recap slicks. Driving this car, Heath won the Top Eliminator title at the 1956 NHRA Championship Drag Races that were held in Kansas City, Missouri. His elapsed time was 10.49 seconds, and his speed was 141.50 miles per hour. Heath ran his car on a mixture of nitromethane and was the last nitro burner to win an NHRA National Championship until 1963.

Following that event, Heath returned to his Oklahoma farm. With the help of his wife, Betty, he started to prepare his car for the 1955 National Drags. He did well with that car, but unfortunately he was scratched from the finals due to an accident along the return road.

Undaunted by his previous year's problems, Melvin Heath returned with a vengeance in 1956. He was the first driver to win two NHRA regional meets in a single season: the Southwest Regional at Caddo Mills, Texas, and the Missouri Valley Regional at Sioux City, Iowa.

On Labor Day weekend, Heath, along with 351 other entrants, made the pilgrimage to Kansas City, Missouri, for the 1956 National Championship Drag Races. The event ran four full days with the finals held on Monday, September 3. Ten thousand fans watched intently as the final two competitors rolled to the line for the run for the Dragster class. In the left lane was Californian Bob Alsenz in his sleek, Chrysler-powered slingshot dragster. In the right lane was Melvin Heath. To qualify for the final, Heath had just beaten the 1955 National Champ, Calvin Rice. The race between Heath and Alsenz was very close. At the end, they didn't know who had won until the track announcer proclaimed, "Class winner . . . *Melvin Heath of Oklahoma!*" The first person to shake Heath's hand was competitor Bob Alsenz.

2

TONY NANCY'S 22JR. ROADSTER

If you were at a newsstand late in 1957 scanning the racks of magazines for something good to read, your eyes might have stopped at the December issue of *Hot Rod* magazine. On the cover of that issue was a red-orange roadster with the number 22*Jr.* on the door. The hood was off, revealing the blown flathead tucked partially under the cowl. Three young men were working on the roadster and one of them was the owner, Tony Nancy.

Tony Nancy carefully crafted the tonneau cover, which hides the passenger compartment on the 1929 Model A Ford roadster body. Cutting large holes in the 1932 Ford frame rails lightened them without sacrificing strength. When this car was built in the mid-1950s, mag wheels were rarely seen on drag racing cars. Most racers did what Nancy did on this roadster and fitted aluminum discs to the stock wheels.
INSET

The Model A's interior was stripped, and a new firewall and floor were crafted from sheet aluminum. Bracing along the sides connects to a small roll bar under the cowl to the larger one over driver Tony Nancy's head. The centrally mounted steering gear is from a 1937 Plymouth. The two smaller chrome bars support the tonneau cover.

PREVIOUS
The rear axle is a combination of 1940 Ford and 1950 Lincoln components with a Halibrand quick-change center section. The fuel tank is under the louver-riddled deck lid.

This flathead engine, built by Tom Sparks, originally powered a Willys coupe that he raced. The engine features an Italmeccanica supercharger with three Stromberg 97 carburetors on top. On a mixture of 50 percent nitro, the little flathead developed enough power to drive Tony Nancy's roadster to quarter-mile speeds of close to 140 miles per hour.

Tony Nancy is a legend in the hot rod world on several levels. But, if you were to meet him on the street, you'd be engaged by his easygoing demeanor and his infectious smile, seemingly unaffected by his own success and notoriety. Since the mid-1950s, Nancy's upholstery, with its trademark Sea Horse logo, has graced the inside of some of the world's best dragsters, boats, custom cars, and hot rods. As a drag racer, he's set several records and has always built innovative and beautiful cars. Each time he's appeared on the cover of *Hot Rod* magazine, it's been with a different race car that he built.

The little roadster on the cover of that December 1957 issue of *Hot Rod* was Nancy's first race car. He was introduced to drag racing by a good friend, Tom Sparks. "I didn't know too much about drag racing other than going a couple of times to watch," says Nancy. "Tom owned a company called Sparks & Bonney Automotive, and he had a Willys coupe with a blown flathead. Tom did very well; his coupe ran very quick and beat a lot of guys. One day Tom came by my shop and I mentioned to him how well his Willys coupe ran and he said, 'If I had a roadster, it would be lighter and would run faster.' Then he said, 'Why don't you build a roadster, and I'll put my engine in it and we'll go racing.' So I said, OK."

Nancy set about to build what has since become the quintessential hot rod—a 1929 Ford Model A roadster body on a pair of 1932 Ford frame rails. Or, in hot rod lingo, an A roadster on Deuce rails. "I bought the frame and body separately," says Nancy. "In those days, you could find '29 bodies and '32 rails just about everywhere. Everybody had an old car." Nancy lightened the frame by cutting large holes in the rails. The rear radius rods and brake backing plates were also drilled to lighten the car. A generous amount of finely crafted sheet aluminum was used for the firewall and driver's compartment. The seat and tonneau cover were stitched by Nancy in his Sherman Oaks, California, shop. Sparks' blown flathead engine was installed and they went racing.

Tony Nancy's good friend, Tom Sparks, leans over to give him a few last-minute instructions prior to making a run down the San Fernando Raceway. The light blue 1951 Ford Woody wagon behind the roadster is Nancy's shop car (note lettering on the door). Several changes were made to the roadster by the time it appeared in *Hot Rod* magazine's December 1957 issue. *Dan LaCroix collection*

Strip and class records were broken just about everywhere the roadster ran. It even beat a few dragsters for Top Eliminator titles. The fastest the roadster ran was 10.14 seconds at 138 miles per hour. This was an outstanding time for a 256-cubic inch flathead. "I drove it and we proceeded to win about 130 trophies," says Nancy. "There weren't many Hemis that ran very well then. The ones that were there weren't really killers. We proceeded to run it up and down the coast from San Francisco to San Diego and did very well." After a year of competition, Sparks decided to get out of drag racing and go bicycle racing instead, something he had been doing on the side. Nancy continued racing the car for another year. After he sold it, he began construction on another roadster that would also appear on the cover of *Hot Rod* magazine in August 1962.

The most outstanding feature of Nancy's roadster was the overall quality of workmanship. Very few hot rods built in the late 1950s were constructed with the kind of detail Nancy put into his roadster. Nancy attributes his skills to the early automotive craftsmen he worked for as a kid. When he was 13 years old, Nancy would ride his bike over to several automotive specialty shops after school and hang out. He would occasionally sand a car or do whatever he could to help. The impressions made on Nancy by these early automotive craftsmen have stuck with him for life. "They didn't try and see how fast they could do it—they tried to see how well they could do it," says Nancy. "When you're young, your environment is what molds you. This dedication to quality probably just rubbed off on me. Later, when I built my own car, I tried to incorporate what I'd learned into the construction. I was very fortunate that people thought my cars looked nice." Nancy also has a great deal of respect and admiration for his friend Tom Sparks, whom he considers his mentor. "He's the guy who taught me about drag racing," says Nancy. "He taught me how to drive and he taught me how to build. His work was always very sanitary. Everything I accomplished was as a result of Tom."

3

DON GARLITS' *SWAMP RAT 1*

In 1950 when Don Garlits made his first pass down the converted air strip in Zephyrhills, Florida, in his 1940 Ford, he was simply known as Don Garlits. He wasn't Big Daddy, King Rat, Mr. Rear Engine, Tampa Dan, or Big. He was just Don Garlits, and he didn't even have the fastest car. What Don did have back then (and still has now) was an innovative mind. "They didn't have my mind," says Garlits. "That's the only difference that's ever been. We all have the same two hands and I'm certainly not stronger than anybody. But I can think—and I dare to think for myself.

The fat whitewalls on the slicks weren't for show. Racing slicks in the 1950s were made by recapping soft rubber over the tread of a worn-out tire. In this case, the tires used were whitewalls. The small tires on the front are from a motorcycle.
INSET

The engine in Don Garlits' *Swamp Rat 1* is a 392-cubic inch Chrysler Hemi with an Isky cam. The eight Stromberg 97 carburetors sit on top of an aluminum Weiand Drag Star manifold. Both Ed Iskenderian and Weiand touted Garlits' accomplishments in their magazine advertisements. The sheet metal covering the carburetors prevents fuel from being siphoned out of the carburetors when the car is at speed.

The *Swamp Rat 1* was built in 1956, but it wasn't until the summer of 1958 that Garlits started receiving notoriety for his drag racing accomplishments. Exhaust header technology for dragsters in the 1950s was in its infancy. Garlits added these long swept-back headers, commonly called "weed burners," because he liked their racy looks.

skillful with his hands and racing on a limited budget. Painted purple with Don's Garage & Speed Shop on the nose, Garlits was ready to take on the world with his new dragster.

Out of the box, Garlits was pleased with the performance of his new dragster. He was Top Eliminator at the Florida State Championships with an elapsed time of 10.9 seconds and a speed of 135 miles per hour. For the 1957 season, Garlits changed the intake manifold to a Weiand Drag Star aluminum manifold mounting eight Stromberg 97 carburetors. The nose was also modified, creating a lower, more streamlined profile. Finally, the car was painted a sinister shade of black with red and white pinstriping.

In August 1957, the AATA (American Automobile Timing Association) was holding its Fourth Annual World Series of Drag Racing in Cordova, Illinois. Earlier in the year, the NHRA had banned the use of nitromethane, but other sanctioning bodies, like the AATA, allowed it. Most of the top dragster owners and drivers were addicted to the additional speed the nitro gave them and competed in events that allowed them to use exotic fuels. Such was the case of the Cordova meet, where two of the biggest names of the day in dragsters appeared, Cook & Bedwell and Setto Postoian. This was Garlits' first big meet out of his home state of Florida, and he was in awe of some of his competitors about whom he'd read in the pages of *Hot Rod* magazine. Garlits was eliminated by Postoian who went on to win the event. Though eliminated, Garlits left Cordova knowing he could run with the big dogs.

It was also at the 1957 Cordova meet that Garlits started running higher percentages of nitro (up to 95 percent). This required some changes in the way he ran the car. He found that prior to the run, the engine needed to be fully up to temperature to accept the volume of fuel it was about to receive. "When you come to the starting line, what you're wanting is temperature," says Garlits. "So you blip the throttle and you're lettin' it run." As the temperature increased, Garlits would pull closer to the starting line. In 1957, there were no staging lights or Christmas tree. Someone would assist the cars approaching the starting line and the race would be started by the flagman who stood in the center of the track. "On this particular car, one of the things you had to do was get an awful lot of fuel to get it to pull in high gear," says Garlits. "Remember, there's no supercharger." Garlits had a small hand pump mounted on the differential that he used to pressurize the fuel tank. "You'd pump up the fuel pressure till it reached 10 pounds. With 10 pounds, the floats in the carburetors begin to sink and the engine floods. That additional fuel will cause the engine to pop—that means it's ready to go!"

Now it was up to the starter to get the competitors off. The starter would hold the flag in one hand with the tip touching the ground. As soon as the flag was lifted, the race was on. "The minute you saw that flag twitch—you'd better be out of there," says Garlits. "I'd watch the starter's arm, and when I saw the muscle in his arm give that little quiver—I let it go, because I knew he was fixin' to pull the flag."

Early dragster races were tire-smoking events. About midcourse, the smoke would clear as the speed of the car caught up to the speed of the rotating tires. "By the seat of your pants is how you drove it," says Garlits. "You're moving the wheel around according to how it's movin'. Pretty soon the smoke starts to dry up and you can see the tires. Now it's on the way pretty good." Because of the large volume of fuel required during the run, Garlits had to continue pumping additional pressure into the fuel system while driving a straight course down the strip. As the speed increased, he would tuck his head down out of the wind stream. As he headed through the lights, he'd back off, push in the clutch, and shut the fuel off. "It was exciting because it lasted a long time and there was a lot to do," says Garlits.

In 1958, Garlits took the *Swamp Rat 1* back to Cordova and set the top speed of the event at 172.08 miles per hour. The following week, he took Top Eliminator at the American Hot Rod Association (AHRA) Nationals at Great Bend, Kansas. Garlits continued his rampage with *Swamp Rat 1* by winning the Texas State Championships at Caddo Mills, Texas. Garlits' racing exploits in 1958 were exuberantly tracked by car sponsor Ed Iskenderian's copy writers in his advertisements for camshafts.

Garlits' notoriety was a sore spot for the California drivers who felt many of his record times were measured on inaccurate clocks. This discord set the stage for a West Coast showdown. On March 1, 1959, Garlits made his appearance at the Bakersfield, California, Fuel and Gas Championships. Garlits' car was not running very well, and he was soundly defeated in the first round. This defeat, along with the gibes of the competitors and spectators, was especially painful for Garlits to accept. As the world would learn, it's not nice to laugh at Don Garlits. It only makes him more determined.

Many of the competitors at Bakersfield were running superchargers on their Chrysler engines. The performance of the supercharged cars was far superior to the unsupercharged cars, like Garlits' *Swamp Rat 1*. Following that event, Garlits knew he had to make the conversion. Two weeks later, Garlits arrived at Kingdon, Arizona, with a 671 blower sitting atop his Chrysler engine. Here, Garlits got his revenge. He continued to race the *Swamp Rat 1* through 1960. In 1961, *Swamp Rat II* and *Swamp Rat III* appeared, starting a long line of record-breaking dragsters.

4

MOONEYHAM
554 FUEL
COUPE

When drag racing started in California, the strips were filled with scores of hot rods, primarily 1930s vintage Ford roadsters and coupes with hopped-up engines. Many of these cars also competed on the dry lakes. Such is the story of the Mooneyham & Sharp 554 coupe.

In the 1950s, Gene Mooneyham had a full-fendered, flathead-powered 1934 Ford sedan that he raced on the dry lakes, running as fast as 120 miles per hour. He also ran it at

The Mooneyham coupe, also known as the 554 coupe, looks like a traditional street rod without headlights. It carries all the classic lines of the 1934 Ford coupe on which it's based. The only alteration to the five-window body was the removal of 3 1/2 inches from the roof line.
INSET

The inside of the Mooneyham coupe is race-car stark. The firewall and floor pan are made from sheet aluminum. The driver's seat is dead center and moved as far rearward as possible. On the right, the large "Moon" accelerator pedal has a metal band across the top. This allowed the driver to shut the throttle if a return spring broke. Just to the right of the accelerator is the foot brake, which is also connected to the hand brake lever. The clutch is to the left side of the steering column. Coming up along the A-pillars and connecting above the driver's seat is the sturdy network of roll bar tubing.

The engine's long individual exhaust headers can be seen under the door. Driver Larry Faust claims it was exceptionally loud inside, as the sound of the engine was amplified by the aluminum floor pan.

be challenged by any of the lesser cars, but the race was run on the track chosen by the number-one car. When challenged, Mooneyham was smart enough to know which tracks were best for his car and not so good for his challenger. The Mooneyham coupe was a big draw and it has been rumored that a few of the tracks made some "errors" in timing to keep the coupe above the nine-second mark.

In 1963, Mooneyham had the desire to move on to dragsters and sold the coupe to Emmitt Smith for $3,500. The price included the trailer and a brand-new set of aluminum heads. Mooneyham told Smith that the coupe would run quicker than nine seconds anytime he wanted, but Smith doubted it. Mooneyham also warned him that if he did run quicker than 9.0, he'd be out of the Jr. Eliminator program. This warning didn't sink in. The first run Faust made for Smith was 8.9 seconds at Lions Drag Strip in Long Beach, California. This immediately removed the coupe from the Jr. Eliminator list. Smith then asked how fast the coupe really was. The usual 60 to 70 percent of nitro was increased considerably and Faust took it to the line. During that pass down the strip, the engine exploded. "When it blew, it kicked the rods out and then the fuel tank exploded!" exclaims Faust. "There was fire comin' out the back window of that thing. I opened the door and was ready to jump because it was too hot in there. About that time, the fire died down and I stayed in the car." New owner Smith only got one and a half runs out of the car. "It was pretty simple," snickers Faust. "Gene got paid Saturday morning, and I blew it up on Saturday night!"

5

ALBERTSON OLDS DRAGSTER

The Albertson Olds was a gas dragster owned by Gene Adams and Ronnie Scrima. Scrima was an early pioneer of dragsters and Adams, who started out racing his dad's 1950 Olds fastback, handled the wrenches on the supercharged Olds engine. Selected to drive was Leonard Harris from Playa del Rey, California. Harris had a solid reputation as an excellent driver and brought to the team a sponsorship from a local Oldsmobile dealer.

The frame was a modified Chassis Research K-88. Chassis Research was the first company to commercially produce dragster frames and was very successful, producing hundreds of chassis. In the late 1950s, Scotty Fenn, owner of

The summer of 1960 was an amazing year for the Albertson Olds team. They ran a string of 12 consecutive wins at Lions Drag Strip and ended the summer with the Top Eliminator win at the NHRA Nationals.
INSET

Gene Adams built a stout 462-cubic inch Olds engine for the Albertson Olds dragster. The supercharger is a GMC 671 and Hilborn four-port injectors sit on top. The Albertson Olds ran on gasoline, because nitromethane fuel had been banned by the NHRA three years earlier.

The frame for the Albertson Olds is a modified Chassis Research K-88. Chassis Research was one of the first and most successful commercial dragster chassis builders. These frames featured a very short wheelbase and an extremely rugged construction.

Chassis Research, was a controversial figure and had his own unique theories on dragster chassis construction. One of these theories was that the wheelbase of a dragster should be equal to the circumference of the rear tire. This resulted in very short wheelbase frames (92 inches), at a time when the trend was toward longer wheelbase dragsters.

Leonard Harris, driver of the Albertson Olds, owned a Los Angeles-area gas station and had a reputation as a street racer. Although he was relatively small in stature at five feet, seven inches, Harris was very well built. He was a former gymnast who had won two National Championships on steel rings. The attributes needed to be a top gymnast are strength, concentration, and coordination—the same attributes needed to drive a dragster.

When Harris drove the Albertson Olds, he sat low in the seat with his head cocked to the left as he looked around the blower. His right hand was at the twelve o'clock position on top of the butterfly steering wheel, and his left hand was at the six o'clock position. Harris knew how to win races. He either beat his competitor off the line, or outran them at the top end. The customary dragster run in 1960 included clouds of smoke from the slicks, as the driver dumped the clutch at the start. Harris developed a method of slipping the clutch just enough to avoid smoking the tires. This technique produced some very quick elapsed times.

In May 1960, Adams built a new 462 cubic-inch engine for the dragster. It featured an Engel cam, a GMC 671 blower, and Hilborn injectors. During the summer of 1960, the Albertson Olds amassed a string of 12 consecutive Saturday-night victories at the Lions Drag Strip in Long Beach, California. On Sunday, the Albertson team would travel to one of the other Southern California drag strips and handily whip the competition.

As the 1960 NHRA U.S. Nationals were drawing near, most pundits were predicting that a twin-engine dragster would win it all. Many twins were running at the time and several of the teams had figured out the unique combination. Detroit area twin driver Donnie Westerdale was entered, and Californian Tommy Ivo brought his twin Buick-powered rail. The Dragmaster team of Dode Martin and Jim Nelson also made the trek to the Motor City. Their *Two Thing*, as they called it, set the fastest time of the meet at 171 miles per hour. It was powered by two supercharged 354 cubic-inch Chevy engines.

The Albertson Olds was entered in the tough A Dragster class, which had 36 entries. When the class eliminations were over, the winner was the Albertson Olds. On Monday, the run for Top Eliminator included the AA dragster Dragmaster *Two Thing*, Ray Goodman's A Modified Roadster *Tennessee Bo-Weevil*, and the Albertson Olds. The first round saw the Albertson Olds against the Dragmaster *Two Thing* with Harris winning by a slim margin. Now Harris would have to run against the *Bo-Weevil* that had received a bye in the first round. Goodman's blown Chrysler-powered roadster handily took its class during eliminations and set a national record of 9.97 seconds at 153.84 miles per hour. While not the equal on paper of the Albertson dragster, the speedy roadster couldn't be taken lightly.

When the starter lifted the flag, it was Harris all the way in the Albertson Olds. The Top Eliminator win earned the Albertson team a 1960 Ford station wagon presented by the D-A Lubricant company. Ronny Scrima, crew chief at the Detroit Nationals, was also awarded a gold signet ring from the D-A Lubricant company for the work he did to keep the

It's Labor Day weekend in Michigan. Just south of Detroit, at the corner of Dix and Sibley Roads, the 1960 NHRA National Championship Drag Races are being held at Detroit Dragway. Starter Joe Gutierrez has just lifted the flag and the Albertson Olds, with Leonard Harris driving, is making another run on its way to the Top Eliminator title. *Greg Sharp collection*

This is the view Leonard Harris would have had looking down the drag strip (in this case Pomona) from the seat of the Albertson Olds. He sat in a reclined position with his legs over the rear axle. His right foot was on the large accelerator pedal on the right. His left foot was on the clutch (obscured by the block of wood holding it in the released position). There is no brake pedal. Stopping a dragster is done by hand with the brake lever on the right side of the cockpit. Because of the low seating position and large supercharger, Harris would cock his head to the left so he could see where he was going.

Albertson Olds in top shape during the meet. The Albertson team also won the *Motor Life* magazine award for best elapsed time at 9.25 seconds.

Following the Nationals, Harris picked up where he left off at Lions Drag Strip. On September 24, the Albertson Olds dipped into the eights with a pass of 8.96 seconds at a speed of 171.42 miles per hour. On October 22, 1960, a match race was scheduled at Lions between Harris' Albertson Olds and Howard Johansen's twin Chevy-powered dragster. Although it was billed as

the "Match Race of the Century," it never materialized. The twin Chevy dragster blew one of its engines during a tune-up pass. Harris made a single pass with the Albertson Olds and when he returned to the pits, there was water running out of the engine from a cracked head. Harris took the opportunity to drive the new Firestone Realty dragster. But, in the first round of eliminations, the steering failed and the dragster flipped, killing Harris. Leonard Harris was not the first to die while drag racing, nor would he be the last.

6

EINOLANDER & CANDEE DRAGSTER

Chuck Einolander, Ralph Candee, and Dick Hanson met in high school and were all passionate about drag racing. They drove 1940s-era Ford coupes and would drag race each other on the streets of San Diego. In 1959, it wasn't unusual for teenagers in high school auto shop classes to be daydreaming of drag racing. But, in the late 1950s, these three young men acted on their dream.

The January 1959, issue of *Hot Rod* magazine was of particular interest to them. That issue featured a story on Art Chrisman's *Hustler 1*, one of the top dragsters in the country. "That article told about what he used for main chassis

With a high-revving engine in the front and the driver sitting on top of the differential, it took a great deal of courage to drive a front-engine dragster. The only instrumentation is the small oil pressure gauge mounted on the back of the engine near the distributor.

INSET

In 1963, a blown small-block Chevy engine was installed in the chassis. Legendary racer Mickey Thompson built the short block with a stroker crankshaft that increased the cubic inches to 354. At the same time, the original Model A rear axle was replaced with a stronger Chevy unit.

Drag racing's roots were always in the neighborhood garages of America. Such is the case of the Einolander & Candee dragster, where the dreams of a few young men came true in their home-built dragster.

rails," says Ralph Candee. "I figured if it was good enough for him, it's good enough for me. So, right then I started sketching and I drew some chalk lines on the garage floor. We went to the drag races to take measurements of other dragsters. Pretty soon, we came up with a main chassis rail plan. We went to a

chassis fabrication shop in San Diego and had the main rails built out of 2 1/2-inch mild steel tubing."

They set the rails up on crates in the garage, bought wheels and tires, and continued to buy and make small components for the car. "There wasn't any of this computerized design," says Candee. "If it

was a slump in construction, they would go to the drags to get a shot in the arm.

To shake down the new Einolander-Candee-Hanson dragster, they trailered it to a then-deserted area north of San Diego called Torrey Pines. There they fired it up and were able to determine what they needed to do to get it ready to race. Their goal was to compete in the B Dragster class at the 1961 Bakersfield Fuel and Gas Championships. They missed that date by one month, with the car's first run at Pomona, in April 1961. When the dragster was first built, it had an unblown 391-cubic inch Olds engine that ran on gas. It had a two-speed Cad LaSalle transmission and a Model A Ford rear end with Model A brakes. "In those days, that was cool," says Candee with a smile.

Ralph Candee fondly remembers his first time down the strip in the car. "I'd never gone more than a hundred miles an hour in the quarter before, and here I just turned one-thirty. I blinked once—and I was in the other lane. It was a good thing I was on the track alone! I shut it down like they say you do in a dragster. You throw in the clutch and start on the brakes. What they didn't tell me is that you pump the brakes to stop. Well, I saw that I was eatin' up a lot of track real fast, so I leaned on the brakes to get stopped. By the time I stopped and turned around, the smoke was just curlin' out of those things." Dode Martin, a top dragster driver of the day, made a pass with the Dragmaster *Two Thing* right behind Candee. After he got his car turned around at the end of the strip, and seeing the smoke coming off of the brakes on Candee's car, Martin asked Candee what technique he was using to get his car stopped. Martin then explained to Candee the proper method of stopping a dragster.

In 1962, team member Dick Hanson's move to Washington state split the three-way partnership. Hanson took the Olds engine with him and eventually built another dragster around it. Candee and Einolander were left with the chassis and trailer.

looked good, it probably was good." They kicked around the design of the roll cage quite a bit. "We sort of married the Scotty Fenn roll cage to the *Hustler 1* frame rails," says Candee. "It was something we preferred." To determine the height of the roll cage, one of the trio sat within the frame rails in a driving posture. "Once the roll cage went on, it was all go from there," says Candee. From then on, it was just a matter of buying parts. Whenever there

The design of the frame for the Einolander &
Candee dragster was a combination of the best
of several commercial chassis available in the late
1950s. It featured a very short wheelbase, a low
profile, and a sturdy roll bar design.

Racing in A Dragster class, the Einolander &
Candee dragster makes a pass down the fabled
Lions Drag Strip. Lions was a favorite drag strip of
many Southern California competitors. It was there
that Chuck Einolander turned a best for the
Einolander & Candee dragster at 161.5 miles per
hour in 10.01 seconds. *Chuck Einolander collection*

They decided to install a blown small-block Chevy.
"We could have put in a stock Chevy with injectors,"
says Candee. "But, *no*—we had to do better than
that." They bought a Mickey Thompson-built short
block and a brand-new set of Corvette fuel injection
heads. They took the heads to Dragmaster, a local

high-performance shop owned by Dode Martin and
Jim Nelson, and had them ported and polished. "We
bought a Crankshaft Company stroker crank, which
boosted the cubic inches from 283 to 354," says
Candee. "This was big time back then!" A 671 GMC
blower was added with Hilborn four-port injectors.
The fragile Model A rear end was replaced with a late
model Chevy and the transmission was removed,
converting the car to direct drive.

These changes took quite a bit of money and time
and it wasn't until February 1963, that they were back
on the track with the Einolander & Candee dragster. "It
wasn't running good at all," confides Candee. "We had
a lot to learn about blown engines. In March 1963, we
went to the Fuel and Gas Championships at
Bakersfield, where the blown engine put us in the A
Dragster class. Four days later, I was in the Army."

Chuck Einolander was now on his own with the
dragster. One evening, he got together with Martin and
Nelson from Dragmaster, and found out both the mag-
neto and fuel injectors needed adjustments. This boosted the performance considerably and quarter-mile
speeds increased to 160 miles per hour. This increase in
speed caught Einolander by surprise and, like Candee's
eventful first ride, Einolander had his own episode at the
end of the track. Luckily, there was no serious damage
as the dragster's body did its best imitation of an earth
mover and scraped up a few pounds of dirt as it ground
to a halt. Einolander got a handle on the car and ran a
best time of 161.5 miles per hour in 10.01 seconds at
Lions Drag Strip in Long Beach, California.

Late in 1963, Chuck Einolander was also
inducted into the Army. Following their discharge
a few years later, Candee and Einolander let their
dragster sit until 1969 when they decided to go
racing again, this time without a blower. They took
it to the 1970 Bakersfield March meet. When they
started it up, the engine didn't have any oil pressure. They shut it off, and that was the last time the
Einolander & Candee dragster saw a race track.

CHAPTER 7

JACOBSON'S
1962
CHEVY 409

There was no doubt in 1962 which car was king of the Super Stock battles—the 409 Chevy. At the 1962 NHRA Winternationals, Don Nicholson handily won the Stock Eliminator title. Later in the year at the U.S. Nationals, Hayden Proffitt took home the NHRA Stock Eliminator honors—both were driving 409 Chevys. The 409 Chevys were inexpensive and, when tuned properly, were race winners. A new 1962 Chevy with a 409 engine and a

Tom Jacobson worked for Gledhill Chevrolet in Wilmington, California, and convinced them to sponsor him. Another sponsor was Hayden Proffitt, who owned a high-performance shop in nearby Garden Grove.

INSET

In 1962, the Chevy Biscayne was the least expensive and lightest model in the full-size Chevrolet lineup. Its interior reflected the Biscayne's low-cost image with inexpensive trim. Without a heater or radio, the Jacobson's Biscayne is typical of 1960s-era super stockers. The Sun tachometer, standard with the 409 engine, has been moved up from the steering column to the top of the instrument panel. The original four-speed shift linkage has been replaced with a Hurst Competition Plus unit. An aftermarket oil pressure gauge has been mounted at the base of the steering column where an optional clock would have been located.

Powering the Jacobson's 1962 Biscayne is a 409 cubic-inch engine with Chevrolet's optional Z-11 heads and a high-rise intake manifold. The AHRA allowed the 1962 Chevys competing in stock classes to run these components even though they were only available at the Chevrolet parts counter. The exhaust headers were built by Jacobson when they bought the car.

four-speed transmission could be purchased for as little as $2,800. This included a 12-month, 12,000-mile warranty that had no exclusions for racing.

Out on the West Coast, 16-year-old Butch Leal had convinced his parents to buy him a 409 Chevy so he could go drag racing. What Mom and Pop Leal bought for their son was the cheapest and lightest body style Chevrolet had to offer—a two-door Biscayne sedan. Under the hood was a 409-cubic inch engine with twin four-barrel carburetors, rated at 409 horsepower. A close-ratio four-speed transmission, positraction rear axle, and Sun tachometer were the only options added. No frills like a radio or heater were needed for quarter-mile drives.

Leal campaigned his Biscayne in the NHRA Super Stock class on the West Coast throughout the 1962 season. He was very successful and picked up the nickname, "The California Flash." At the end of the year, Leal took delivery of a 1963 Z-11 Impala and put the 1962 Biscayne up for sale. When Tom

Jacobson and his wife, Linda, found out the car was available, they were interested. The Jacobsons knew of the car and how successful it had been. Tom was working for Gledhill Chevrolet in Wilmington, California, and convinced the owners of the dealership to sponsor him if he were to buy the car. They agreed to a sponsorship arrangement where Tom would receive parts and time off to race, if they painted Gledhill Chevrolet on the side of the car. As it turned out, time off was the most important component of the deal. For $1,900 the Jacobsons got the car and the keys, but none of Leal's speed secrets.

Another sponsor of the Jacobsons' sedan was Hayden Proffitt & Associates Performance Shop. They initially went to Proffitt because he was a top runner with his own 409. Proffitt did the valve jobs on their 409 and, before long, he and the Jacobsons became fast friends. Tom took the Biscayne to Jim Dugan's muffler shop in Willmington, California, and built his own tri-y exhaust headers.

The Jacobsons raced their Biscayne every Wednesday, Friday, Saturday, and Sunday in the Southern California area. They became fixtures at the nearby Lions Drag Strip. "Lions was our home track," says Linda. "We could hear that track from our house. If you wanted to find us on a Saturday night—all you had to do was go to Lions." The Jacobsons ran their Biscayne through 1963 and 1964, configured for NHRA's A-stock class, running elapsed times as low as 12.30 seconds. Whenever Butch Leal's mom asked Butch how his old 1962 was doing, she always referred to the car as "Old Blue." This reference to the car stuck and the name *Old Blue* was soon lettered on the Biscayne's C-pillar.

The Jacobsons ran their last NHRA event in 1964. On the Wednesday prior to the NHRA's U.S. Nationals in Indianapolis, there was a big meet held in Muncie, Indiana. Forty-nine A-stockers unloaded for the event with only two of the big names (Bill Jenkins and Don Gay) not participating. Jacobson handily won the event.

Tom Jacobson leans into the engine compartment to check the carburetor linkage on his Chevy's dual quad carburetors. The red jacket he's wearing is an original Class Winner jacket he won at Lions Drag Strip.

That weekend at the Nationals, while in the staging lanes awaiting their turn to run, the Jacobsons' car was protested by the team of Joe Gardner, Arnie Waldman, and Joe Tryson, who were also running a 409 Chevy A-stocker named *Northwind*. Their claim was that the Jacobsons' car was missing some front bumper bracing. Since they obtained the car from Leal, the Jacobsons had not removed any bracing, adding only two small tow bar brackets. This is the way they had run the car at NHRA events for the year and a half prior to the Nationals and had never been protested. The protest stood and they were not allowed to participate in the biggest race of the year. "We protested *Northwind* and they were thrown out, too," says Linda. As it turns out, there wasn't a winner in the A-stock class that year due to protests. "It was the most memorable and last time we ran an NHRA event with that car," says Tom.

The Jacobsons began running AHRA (American Hot Rod Association) events. The AHRA's rules for A-stock were a little more lenient than those of the NHRA. This allowed them to run the new Z-11 high-rise intake manifold and heads. The AHRA also allowed cam changes, and Jacobson installed a specially ground cam by Sig Erson. With the new cam, Jacobson was now turning times in the high 11s. Jacobson's *Old Blue* ran only at AHRA events through 1965 and 1966, setting several records along the way. By the time they retired *Old Blue* in 1966, it was running the quarter-mile in 11.50 seconds at 120 miles per hour.

Recently, while attending a drag race as spectators, the Jacobsons were recognized by a former competitor. They struck up a conversation about the old days, and he confessed that he purposely avoided the tracks when the Jacobsons ran *Old Blue*—just so he could have a chance.

8

MELROSE MISSILE III 1963 PLYMOUTH SUPER STOCK

In 1962 Charlie Di Bari was home, fresh from a tour flying jets in the Air Force. Di Bari was working at Melrose Motors, a Plymouth dealership in Oakland, California, owned by his father since 1952. In the early 1960s, Plymouths were best known as taxicabs and family sedans. Di Bari was familiar with the local drags and was also aware of the fact that Chevrolets dominated. One day he sat down and penned a letter to one of the Chrysler vice presidents, Harry Chesebrough, back in

Starting on February 22, 1963, Chrysler released its lightweight front end package for the Plymouth Super Stock cars. It included aluminum front fenders and hood. These parts, along with other weight-saving components, reduced the weight of these cars by 140 pounds. The most obvious part of the package was the bodacious hood scoop, also made of aluminum.
INSET

Melrose Motors was an Oakland, California, Plymouth dealership owned by Charlie Di Bari's father. The sponsorship of the race car was Di Bari's idea, but the name *Missile* and the distinctive graphics on the side of the car were his father's inspiration.

The *Melrose Missile* is powered by a 426 cubic-inch Super Stock engine. Today, this engine is commonly called the "Max Wedge." These 425-horsepower engines were easily identified by the large cross-ram intake manifold. Dual Carter AFB carburetors sat on top in a staggered formation. Each carburetor has a velocity stack with a foam rubber gasket that seals it against the bottom of the hood. This allows only cool fresh air from the hood scoop to enter.

Detroit. Di Bari expressed his desire for Chrysler to produce a performance car for the drags that would change the image of the Plymouth product. A few months later, Di Bari received a call from Chesebrough. He stated that they were indeed going to build 200 drag racing cars. The first was going to a group of Plymouth engineers in Detroit who called themselves "The Golden Commandos." And Di Bari was going to get the second Plymouth off the line. "I said, 'That sounds pretty good—send it,'" Di Bari recalls with a laugh. "I was just a young

whipper-snapper, and I told my dad that I had just bought a race car!"

Di Bari formed a partnership with Tommy Grove. Grove was a local racer who had been running at the drags since 1955. In 1958, he and Lefty Mudersbach had one of the fastest twin-engine dragsters around. In 1961, Grove returned to Super Stock class racing a Chevy. "Grove knew that this thing had to be blueprinted," says Di Bari. "I wasn't a mechanic, but I understood what he wanted to accomplish." Di Bari went to his father and asked for $425 for the engine work. "You have to know my father," says Di Bari. "He's an old Italian. He looks at me and says, '$425 and not a penny more.'" When they were putting the car together, they realized that to be competitive, they needed headers, but had no money. "I said, 'Father, we need another $125 for steel tubing headers and Tommy will make them.'" The elder Di Bari replied "$125—and don't ever come back and see me again!"

The new *Melrose Missile* was successful the first time it ran. "The first race my father attended was the State Championships in Lodi, California," says Di Bari. "We had a ball! We won that night, beating all the Corvettes." A few races later, the *Missile* developed some problems and needed a new engine. Di Bari was carefully explaining the problem to his father, remembering the recent admonishment regarding money. When finished, the elder Di Bari said, "That's no good—order another car—we are going to have two cars from here on out." From that time forward, the *Melrose Missile* team consisted of two cars.

When the 1963 season kicked off, the *Melrose Missile* team was ready with their new Plymouth sedan, the *Melrose Missile III*. It was powered by an improved version of the 413-cubic inch Ramcharger engine that powered the 1962 cars. The Ramcharger engine for 1963 displaced 426 cubic inches and was rated at a conservative 425 horsepower. An improved oiling system, new main bearing inserts, and new connecting rods were all added to improve the reliability of the 1963 engines.

The *Melrose Missile III* started the 1963 racing season with the biggest win of all, taking the Super Stock class honors at the 1963 NHRA Winternationals and setting the elapsed time (e.t.) record. Grove's winning time was 12.37 seconds at 114.94 miles per hour. The dominance of the new Chrysler Super Stock engine was apparent by the win in Super Stock Automatic by Bill Hanyon, driving a 1962 Plymouth, and in the Stock Eliminator win by Al Eckstrand in the

In its racing days, the *Melrose Missile* ran with either a three-speed manual transmission or the TorqueFlite automatic. The switch was made depending on the track Charlie Di Bari and Tom Grove were going to run. Today, it's configured with the automatic, which is controlled by the five pushbuttons on the far left side of the instrument panel.

53

In February 1963, the *Melrose Missile III*, with Tom Grove driving, beat all comers in the Super Stock class at the NHRA Winternationals. In doing so, it set both ends of the national record with a 12.00-second e.t. and 118.26 miles per hour. Customarily, the winner would declare his accomplishment somewhere on the car, as Di Bari did along the bottom of the door. In 1963, the Super Stock class rules limited the rear tire to seven inches in width.

Ramcharger's 1963 Dodge. The *Melrose* team once again ran two cars in 1963: the *Melrose Missile III* and the *Melrose Missile IV*. Both Grove and Di Bari shared the driving responsibilities.

The car that Grove raced at the Winternationals had a three-speed manual transmission. Depending on whom they were racing and where they were racing, the *Melrose* team would often switch to the TorqueFlite automatic. Grove was an outstanding mechanic and could make the switch in less than an hour. Gas Rhonda, a top Ford competitor of the day, confided to Di Bari that competitors were discouraged to learn that Grove could switch transmissions so easily.

Early in 1963, Chrysler started to produce their lightweight front-end components for Plymouths and Dodges. The new aluminum fenders, bumpers, and hood with scoop shaved 140 pounds off the already svelte cars. Following the Winternationals, the *Melrose Missile III* was fitted with this package.

Throughout the summer of 1963, the *Melrose Missile* team hammered the competition. At the West Coast season finale at Half Moon Bay, California, Grove, driving the *Missile III*, turned back a large group of competitors in the Super Stock class. In doing so, he set both ends of the NHRA Super Stock record with an elapsed time of 12.00 seconds at 118.26 miles per hour.

The *Missile's* on-track performance increased Melrose Motors' sales of all cars. "We dominated the local scene for selling high-performance cars," says Di Bari. "The young people would just drag their folks into the dealership—there weren't any insurance problems in those days. It was just a question of buying a car."

Di Bari enjoyed his racing days and recently lamented, "It was really fun back in those days—pure fun. Now they race for money, but back then the money wasn't the thing. It was the competition of the Ford, Chevy, and Plymouth gaggles that went on all the time."

9

MALCOLM DURHAM'S 1963 CHEVY Z-11

In 1963, in an effort to rein in the factories, NHRA "Stock" cars were limited to a maximum of 427 cubic inches. This rule followed the 427-cubic inch maximum set by NASCAR to limit what was foreseen as an imminent cubic inch war between the factories. The NHRA also set minimums on the number of high-performance cars produced on the assembly line. This was done to discourage the production of one-off specialty cars in classes for stock cars.

Chevrolet's entry in the 1963 drag wars was the Z-11-optioned Impala. The Z-11 Chevy was a stick of dynamite with a short fuse. It was the

Chevrolet's last hurrah prior to General Motors' adherence to the AMA's (American Manufacturers Association) racing ban was the Z-11-optioned 1963 Impala. Only 57 of these specially equipped Chevrolets were ever built. Most went to professional racers like Malcolm Durham. Durham purchased this Impala from Hicks Chevrolet in December 1962. The Z-11 option cost him an extra $1,237.40 over the base price of the Impala.
INSET

At the base of the steering column on Durham's Impala is a standard Chevrolet tachometer, an option that was added to all high-performance 1963 Chevys.

10

LARSEN FORD 1965 A/FX MUSTANG

Two very significant events happened at Ford Motor Company in 1964. First, they introduced the wildly successful Mustang. Second, they made a commitment to build a group of cars designed specifically for drag racing—the Thunderbolt Fairlanes. Therefore, with the success of the Mustang, it was natural that in 1965, Ford's premier drag racing car should be a Mustang.

In 1964, Ford engineers knew they had their work cut out for them when Chrysler debuted their powerful Hemi engine. Ford was being consistently beaten at both the NASCAR

The Larsen Ford A/FX Mustang never shared the on-track success that some of the other A/FX Mustangs did in 1975. Sponsors soon realized that showmanship was better than speed as a strategy to get customers into the dealership. In 1966, they ran a wheel-standing Econoline pickup called the *Little Yellow Wagon*. INSET

When lettering their A/FX Mustang, the folks at Larsen Ford added a nice touch to the taillights. Like the hood, the deck lid is held down by pins. Inside the trunk was a large battery mounted over the right rear wheel. Even with the heavy 427 engine, the A/FX Mustang has a 50/50 weight distribution.

The public's affection for the new Mustang, combined with Ford's commitment to racing, spawned the A/FX Mustang for drag racing in 1965. Built for Ford Motor Company by Holman and Moody, these little Mustangs terrorized the competition throughout 1965. The American mag wheels on the front were four inches wide and those on the rear, mounting the slicks, were six inches wide.

tracks and at the drag races by the Mopar's free-breathing Hemis. Ford engineers had to do something and do it quick. Bound, like Chrysler, by the 427-cubic inch limit imposed by both NASCAR and NHRA, they knew freer-breathing heads were the answer. Ford designers came up with their version of the Hemi head, but they upped the ante on Chrysler by adding a single overhead camshaft to each side. Officially called the Single Overhead Cam (SOHC) 427, this engine was simply called a "Cammer" by Ford enthusiasts.

Ford started with the same high-riser 427 block it had so much success with in the previous two years. To the top, Ford's engineers added a set of hemispherical heads that each housed a single camshaft. This design, while bulky, was free breathing and revved like crazy. Ford's engineers used the experience they had with overhead cam engines from their Indy program. Their design concept was simple—add a set of free-breathing hemispherical heads to a proven 427-cubic inch short block. But, they advanced the design one step further by adding a single overhead cam to each head. They produced an engine that could rev (up to and over 8,000 rpm) as well as it could breathe.

The new Hemi heads were beautifully designed, each incorporating a single overhead cam. The cams were driven at half the crankshaft speed by a six-foot chain drive. The advantage to

the overhead cam was the elimination of the traditional valve train, which limited the engine's higher rpm range. Atop each head were two rocker shafts with roller cam followers. Sitting atop the engine were a pair of Holley four-barrel carbs fed cool air by a pair of ducts that grabbed fresh air from behind the grille.

In 1965, A/FX vehicle weight was set at a minimum of 3,200 pounds. Ford engineers put the Mustang on a strict diet with extensive use of fiberglass for hood, doors, and front fenders. The rear seat was removed and the windows were made of Plexiglas. To accept the mass of the 10.00-15 M & H Racemaster slicks, the rear wheel wells were enlarged and the rear axle moved forward two inches. The width of the engine overwhelmed the standard Mustang's narrow engine compartment. To make room, Ford engineers removed the spring towers and installed a flat-leaf torsion bar on each side. A sturdy roll cage was installed, and a Sun tachometer was screwed to the top of the instrument panel. A Hurst shifter selected the gears for the four-speed transmission.

NASCAR ruled the new Cammer and its foe, Chrysler's Hemi, illegal for competition for the 1965 season. NHRA was more liberal in its response to factory development and gave the green light to both Ford and Chrysler to run their Hemis in Factory Experimental classes for 1965.

The new Mustang's debut was auspicious. At the season-opening 1965 Winternationals, Bill Lawton won the A/FX class with a run of 10.92 seconds and a top speed of 128.20 miles per hour. Later in 1965, Gas Rhonda, driving a Cammer-powered Mustang, set the A/FX record at 10.43 seconds with a speed of 134.73 miles per hour. One of the FX Mustangs to run in 1965 was this one, sponsored by the Larsen Ford dealership from White Plains, New York. It was originally built with a 427 wedge engine and later upgraded with the 427 Cammer engine.

Under the hood of the A/FX Mustang was the most potent large cubic inch engine Ford ever built—the 427 Cammer. Ford engineers were able to adapt hemispherical heads with a single overhead cam to an existing 427 engine block. The combination produced over 600 horsepower and was able to rev extremely high. The large air intakes behind the grille were connected to two ducts leading to the twin Holley carburetors.

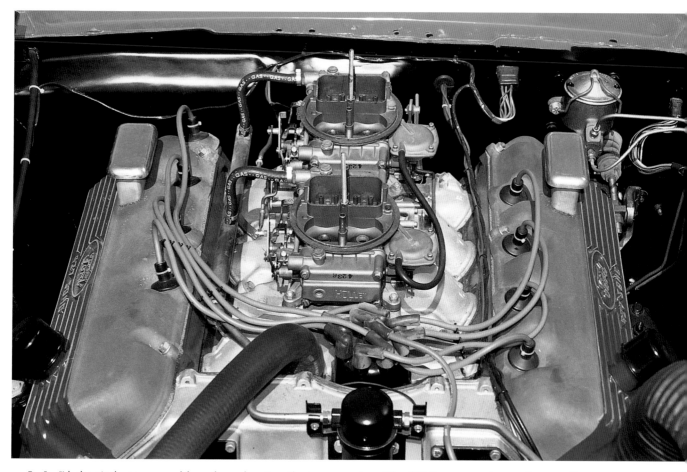

W ith the air ducts removed from the carburetors, the immense size of the 427 Cammer engine can be seen. Two large Holley four-barrel carburetors feed down through an aluminum intake manifold. The valve covers are made of magnesium.

Larsen Ford's driver, Bob Hamilton, ran this Mustang through much of the 1965 season, chasing the tough match race circuit. The folks at Larsen Ford realized if they had an exhibition car like the wheel-standing *Little Red Wagon* and *Hemi Under Glass* they could get as much publicity without all the headaches of match racing. So they built the *Little Yellow Wagon*—a wheel-standing Ford Econoline pickup powered by a Hilborn-injected 427.

By 1966, the "factory" Mustangs took on a new look with an extended front end. Unlike the 1965 models with their Dearborn-built body shell, these cars were custom-built race cars weighing nearly 1,000 pounds less. "Long nose" Mustangs, as they were called, were 1,000 pounds lighter than the 1965 models and ran fuel-injected Cammer engines. The Funny Car era had begun.

CHAPTER 11

MAGICAR TOP FUEL DRAGSTER

In the 1960s, often called the Golden Age of front-engine dragsters, Kent Fuller was one of the premier chassis builders. Fuller, a high school dropout, was highly skilled in metalworking. In 1956 he built quite a reputation as a skilled welder and metal fabricator working for C-T Automotive in North Hollywood, California. In 1958, he struck out on his own, building custom chassis for the growing ranks of drag racers. Drivers like Tommy Ivo, Tony Nancy, Don Prudhomme, and Chris Karamesines lined up to buy his frames. Fuller custom-made each chassis. He made only one spec frame and it sat in his shop for months.

Fuller didn't use any complex jigs or fixtures to fabricate his chassis—they were simply laid out on the floor of his shop in Sherman Oaks,

The *Magicar*, designed by Kent Fuller, was the first dragster to use a small subframe within the car's chassis to support the rear suspension. Up until the time Fuller built this car, dragster rear axles were mounted solidly to the frame.
INSET

Powering virtually every Top Fueler in the mid-1960s was the 392 cubic-inch Chrysler Hemi. The short upswept exhaust headers are called "zoomies."

P art of Fuller's "magic" design was the front suspension. Hidden under the body's needle nose are small rubber isolators that connect the front axle to the frame.

California. Driver ergonomics was a simple matter of Fuller being able to fit in the driver's seat. Most of Fuller's customers wanted a chassis of a proven design and shied away from any experimentation.

Kent Fuller had a dream for a radical new chassis design that would provide an abundance of traction. His design featured a suspended engine and rear axle. Dragsters of that era typically had the engine and rear axle mounted solidly to the frame. Fuller's design placed the engine and rear axle together, supported within an isolated subframe. The subframe was mounted within the car's chassis, and anchored at the front with pivoting isolation mounts. To Fuller, the location of the subframe's front mount to the frame was critical to his design theory. To start with, he carefully located the center of gravity of the engine, clutch, and rear axle assembly. Fuller then located the center of gravity of the chassis with the driver in place. Where these two centers of gravity met was where the front pivoting mount of the subframe would be located. At the rear, the subframe was suspended by an

adjustable coil-spring suspension. The front suspension was also unusual, featuring a pair of small isolators mounted at the very front of the chassis. This unique suspension system gave the 140-inch-long wheelbase frame a high degree of flexibility. The front suspension mounting also lent itself well to the needle-nose bodywork created by Arnie Roberts.

In the market for a dragster at the time were Kaye Trapp, a noted drag racing photographer of the day, and Los Angeles County Sheriff Ron Winkel, who was also an engine builder. They agreed to let Fuller try out his new design on the chassis for their dragster.

The *Magicar* made its debut in October 1964, at Lions Drag Strip. Gathered at the track were chassis builders Woody Gilmore and Roy Steen; both wanted to know if the concept would work as advertised. Fuller was there for the same reason. For the *Magicar's* first pass, owners Winkel and Trapp gave driver Gary Cassiday instructions to shut off before the quarter-mile mark. During that first run, a heavy vibration encouraged driver Cassiday to shut down sooner than expected.

Through the end of 1964, the team fought teething problems with the new chassis design. Too much traction seemed to be the problem. Most dragsters in the mid-1960s had more power than they could apply to the track. The theory behind the *Magicar* combination was to allow the chassis to apply all of the engine's power by isolating the drive-train from the car's chassis. Fuller's theory was apparently working so well that engine builder Winkel had to increase the supercharger output to 21 pounds so the car would smoke the tires.

In January 1965, veteran dragster driver Jeep Hampshire jumped into the *Magicar's* driver seat. "I had known Fuller for years and he must have had some faith in me," says Hampshire. Fuller also theorized that because of the unique frame construction, the rear of the car would lift slightly upon acceleration. Hampshire never noticed that phenomenon. "I know one guy that drove it one time," says Hampshire. "He claimed the engine raised up and that was all he needed—he shut it

The beautiful aluminum body on the *Magicar* was designed and built by Arnie Roberts. Upswept rear body sections on dragsters were very popular at that time. On the *Magicar*, Roberts incorporated a small vertical fin that tapered back from the roll bar to just above the drag chute.

From the driver's seat of a Top Fuel dragster, with over 1,000 trembling horsepower up front, an inferno of nitro flames streaking back from the headers, and two huge rotating slicks on either side boiling the rubber off their surface, the 7.6-second, 200-mile-per-hour ride must have been an incredible experience.

off. By the time I drove it, I didn't let things like that bother me, so I probably didn't even notice."

At the 1965 Bakersfield meet, 64 Top Fuel cars qualified. The *Magicar*, with Hampshire at the controls, qualified 53rd with an elapsed time of 8.03 seconds and a speed of 197.36 miles per hour. Hampshire got the most out of the car, clocking a best elapsed time of 7.62 seconds and a top speed of 204.08 miles per hour. Following Hampshire was driver Gerry Glenn. Glenn's first pass down the strip in the *Magicar* was his first pass *ever* down a drag strip. Glenn was a quick study and, in few years, he would become the NHRA driving champion. During its short year of competition, the *Magicar* won three Top Eliminator trophies.

When dragsters ran in the 1960s, they typically smoked the rear tires for more than half of the quarter-mile run. With the rear tires just starting to smoke, the *Magicar* leaves the starting line at Fontana, California's, Drag City. *Kaye Trapp*

12

MICKEY WEISE'S 1968 HEMI DART

In the late 1960s, Mickey Weise was a brash teenager tearing up the drag strips of Central California in his big-block Camaro. His competitors were sure this young Turk must have been cheating, especially when he set the American Hot Rod Association (AHRA) record for his class at 11.65 seconds and 121.95 miles per hour. He was occasionally beating the factory-sponsored cars and was often protested.

During this time period, Weise became friends and business partners with Harry Holton. Holton had been successfully running a Hemi-powered 1965 Plymouth factory lightweight sedan named the *Hemi Count-Down I.*

When Chrysler Corporation went drag racing in 1968, they combined the smaller Dart body with the powerful Hemi race engine. Chrysler developed the specifications and contracted the Hurst company to build these cars. Extreme weight-saving measures were taken to lighten the cars as much as possible.

INSET

Mickey Weise believes race cars should be raced, and he takes the opportunity to hammer the throttle on his Hemi Dart whenever he can. This car has been running the quarter-mile at speeds over 130 miles an hour for three decades.

Other than its very large hood scoop, the only other obvious modification made to the Dart body was to enlarge the rear wheel openings to fit the slicks. One of the more subtle modifications was the addition of lightweight polymer windows. The gold leaf on the C-pillar was originally added in the late 1960s.

All Hemi Darts were powered by the 426 cubic-inch Chrysler Hemi race engine. It featured 12.5:1 pistons and dual Holly carburetors on a magnesium cross ram intake manifold. The fiberglass hood is held down by competition-style hood pins. An extra pin was added in the front of the hood when Mickey Weise noticed that the hood was beginning to lift at speeds over 110 miles per hour.

Holton helped Weise with his Camaro and constantly tried to get him to switch to a Hemi. "Harry got me interested in the Chrysler thing," recalls Weise. "One day he told me, 'Get in this car and I'll give you a real ride!' He nailed that thing, and it about ripped my head off—it was either switch or lose." In 1968, Chrysler asked them if they wanted one of the special Hemi Darts they were building. "We bought it from Dennis Dodge in Turlock, California," says Weise. "It was a special order that cost about $5,500. The only requirement was to letter 'Northern California Dodge Dealers' somewhere on the car."

The Hemi Dodge Darts and Plymouth Hemi Barracudas were the brain-child of Chrysler's Dick Maxwell. Maxwell was a Chrysler engineer and Ramcharger club member. He felt the powerful Hemi engine in the smaller A-bodied Darts and Barracudas would make unbeatable drag cars. There was a considerable amount of discussion within Chrysler as to whether these cars should be built or not. A few people felt that because there was not a Hemi-powered Dart or Barracuda available to the general public, getting the approval to produce these special cars would be a tough sell to management. The naysayers underestimated the then-current muscle car

The interior of Mickey Weise's Hemi Dart is all original, except for a new carpet, Simpson seat belts, and an Auto Meter tachometer. Weise's Dart is equipped with a TorqueFlite automatic, but Hemi Darts were also built with four-speed manual transmissions. The T-handle on the Hurst shifter was installed by Weise in 1969.

boom and Chrysler's dedication to racing. The project was approved.

Chrysler engineer Bob Tarrozi developed the specifications and built the prototype Barracuda. Both the Barracuda and Dart were built on the same platform. Therefore, the modifications made to shoehorn the big Hemi engine into the prototype Barracuda would be identical for the Dart. The most serious of these modifications was the reworking of the front spring towers and the special brake master cylinder. The balance of the modifications were intended to reduce the car's weight. The front fenders, hood, and oversize scoop were made of fiberglass. The body panels and bumpers were acid dipped to reduce the thickness of the metal. Deleted from the interior were heater, radio, rear seat, all body insulation, and sound-deadening material. The two small bucket seats were added from a Dodge van. All of the windows were made from a lightweight polymer. The quarter-windows were fixed closed and the door windows were raised and lowered with a strap, instead of a crank-type window mechanism.

Chrysler contracted with the Hurst Corporation to fabricate 50 Dodge Darts and 50 Plymouth Barracudas to be built in the initial production run. Hurst opened a special facility in Hazel Park, Michigan, just to build these cars. Later, an additional 25 of each car were produced, bringing total production for each car to 75. Some sources claim the Hemi Dart production totaled 83.

Powering the Hemi Dart is Chrysler's famous race hemispherical-head engine, which featured 12.5:1 pistons, dual Holly carburetors on a magnesium cross ram intake manifold, an aluminum water pump, and Hooker exhaust headers. The Hemi Darts were built with both TorqueFlite automatic and four-speed transmissions.

All of the Hemi Darts were shipped to the dealers with primer covering the metal body panels and the fiberglass front clip components in an unpainted gel coat. The tires and wheels on the car, when delivered, were not raceworthy, and a set of five-spoke Cragar mags were fitted with racing slicks in the back. A roll bar was installed by Turlock Muffler in Turlock, California.

In 1972, Mickey Weise intended to paint his Hemi Dart candy apple red. The white side panel was painted, and a gold base coat was laid down. But before Weise had a chance to paint on the red color coat, he was on his way to another race. Weise decided to leave the car gold, because he felt it would look too much like the *Red Light Bandit*, another car that was running at the time. *Les Welch*

Initially, Holton drove the Hemi Dart, which he named the *Hemi Count-Down II*, with Weise taking over the 1965 Plymouth Hemi sedan. The first time Weise drove that car was at Vernalis, a small converted airport drag strip outside of Modesto, California. "When I got in that '65 Plymouth for the first time, it was like a big long dinosaur," says Weise. "I pointed it and hit it!" On that first run, Weise got on and off of the throttle twice, but still ran a decent 11.20 seconds and 118 miles per hour. Confides Weise, "My first thought was—I don't like this car." Weise eventually got comfortable with the 1965 Hemi and ran it until mid-1969 when he and Holton switched cars.

"I got in the Dart and it just fit me perfectly," recalls Weise. "I told Harry, 'You buy me out of

the business and I'll buy you out of the car—I'll do the racing and you run the shop.' We did that in 1971." In 1972, the side of the car was repainted with the name Mickey Weise. The best time Weise remembers running in the Hemi Dart was 10.19 seconds at 132 miles per hour. In 1973, Chrysler pulled the plug on their support, and that's when Weise put the car away and went back to school.

Mickey Weise's 1968 Hemi Dart has not been restored. Luckily, the car has not been cut up or modified, as so many early race cars have been. This Hemi Dart is not a museum piece, either. Weise makes regular passes down the drag strip with it. And when he does, he has an ear-to-ear grin on his face.

13

MIKE KUHL'S TOP FUEL DRAGSTER

"I drove down my first drag strip in 1954," says Mike Kuhl. "It was in Alton, Illinois." Kuhl was born and raised in St. Louis, Missouri, and was very interested in cars. "I grew up in high school, racing cars," recalls Kuhl. "I started with an old gas coupe and just worked my way up." In 1962, Kuhl moved from St. Louis, Missouri, to Long Beach, California, the home of Lions Drag Strip. At that time, the Lions' culture was heavily saturated with dragsters. "I kind of grew into the dragster thing," says Kuhl, "and starting racing them in '64 or '65."

"This is the last front-motor car I had," says Kuhl. "It's a Woody Gilmore chassis that was built in 1968. It replaced another Woody car

Running a dragster in the late 1960s could be profitable. Many of the Southern California tracks held weekly open dragster shows that paid as much as $1,000. With this kind of money available, Mike Kuhl was able to earn a living from such winnings, without a major sponsor.

INSET

The superchargers used in the 1960s were unmodified units directly off GMC diesels. The hardware on the front of the pulley is the attachment for a removable aircraft electric starter.

Mike Kuhl owned and ran this Woody Gilmore-chassised dragster from 1968 until 1970. The aluminum body was built by Tom Hanna, and the striking paint was applied by George Cerney. The long nosepiece was not a standard fixture on all dragsters. It was an extra-cost item that didn't help performance, but improved the appearance.

that crashed at Long Beach on a Saturday night." Garwood "Woody" Gilmore was a premier dragster chassis builder from the mid-1960s through the mid-1970s. From his Race Car Engineering Shop in Long Beach, California, Gilmore designed and built dragster chassis. Gilmore felt dragster chassis should be flexible, allowing the car to deflect under acceleration and transfer traction-aiding weight to the rear wheels, while keeping the front wheels on the ground. "Back then, his cars were as state-of-the-art as anything you'd buy today," says Kuhl. "One of the unique things about them was that all the parts were interchangeable with almost anybody else's car. The basic parts, like front ends and rear ends, could be swapped." At the time, very few chassis builders considered the benefits of interchangeable components.

"I drove all my own cars up until I got the dragsters," says Kuhl. "I took a few futile attempts at it, but I wasn't good at all. I couldn't concentrate well enough and the engine was throwin' too much crap at me—I didn't think that was a bit fun." Over the years Kuhl used a series of drivers in his dragsters. Carl Olson was Kuhl's partner and the driver of this car.

"We raced three to four nights a week, including Saturdays and Sundays at half a dozen tracks around

In the 1960s, tearing down the engine of a dragster between each round was unheard of. Mike Kuhl would go as many as four races before he disassembled his engine. Kuhl built his engines for reliability and claimed he would outlast anyone. In the two years that Kuhl raced this car, several drivers drove it, with Carl Olson being the last.

Southern California," says Kuhl. "Every Saturday night at Lions they had an eight-car open show. There would be 25 to 30 Top Fuel dragsters qualifying for eight spots. Back then, it was $1,000 to win, which was good money!" Kuhl and Olson would often win at Lions on Saturday night and then make the Sunday race at San Fernando and win there, too. In the late 1960s, it took only two or three guys to take care of the car. Finding a few more people at the track to help was always easy.

"Tearing down between rounds was almost unheard of back then," says Kuhl. "We'd change oil, screw in some plugs, and then add the nitro." Kuhl admits that the old Chrysler Hemis were durable, because they weren't putting the same stresses on them that today's Top Fuel dragsters endure. "We used to run 90 to 95 percent nitro back then. The 671 blowers were basically stock, right off a diesel. You didn't have the load requirements like you do now, because the tires weren't that great, the clutches weren't that great, and, as a matter of fact, neither were the tracks." The biggest problem with the old Chrysler Hemi blocks was that they were susceptible to cracking. "The longevity factor was pretty good," says Kuhl. "We were known for going three or four races without ever tearing the engine apart. The basis of our operation was reliability and durability. We always said we would outlast everybody."

Kuhl admits that no one really knew why engines worked so well on nitromethane. "We had no idea what the nitro did or how it worked," says Kuhl. "It was years before people figured it out. We just knew that you'd go down to Mickey Thompson's to get it. It was $3.75 a gallon back then. You bought five gallons and it would last you

A small wheelie bar was installed on the rear of the frame, just in case the slicks took too big a bite at the start. The "Donkeys" referred to on the back of the seat pan were the unpaid helpers who regularly assisted with the car at the strip.

a whole weekend. It made the cars sound good, look good, and run good. The fans loved the sound, smell, and fire." It was years before technology would allow competitors to place on-board computers to analyze the dynamics of a Top Fuel dragster. "The only indication of how the car was running was the time slip," says Kuhl. "You had to pay attention to it!"

Kuhl and Olson didn't do a lot of traveling with their dragster. They won various Southern California NHRA points meets and regularly competed at the Winternationals. In 1969, they also competed at the U.S. Nationals in Indianapolis and the Spring Nationals in Dallas, Texas. "For the NHRA events," says Kuhl, "you basically got a trophy. We did get a little money from some of the sponsors. Back then, if you were fairly good at it, you didn't have a hard time keeping a race car going. The manufacturers would give you just about anything. We used to get free tires, oil, clutches—you name it. Product came to you pretty well."

Kuhl's dragster was one of the most beautiful on the strip. Its aluminum body was built by Tom Hanna and the striking paint was done by George Cerny. Most of the Top Fuel cars in the 1960s had short bodies that surrounded the driver, leaving nothing forward of the engine but the fuel tank. The long nosepiece was merely cosmetic and didn't increase the performance of the car.

"I think the best this car ever ran was a 6.40 up to as much as 230 miles an hour," says Kuhl. "I remember a couple of times this car ran over 230, but 200 was an excellent run out of something like this." Kuhl sold this car in 1970 and went to a new rear-engine dragster, also a Woody Gilmore car.

79

CHAPTER 14

PETE ROBINSON'S *TINKER TOY VI*

In 1961, the NHRA U.S. Nationals moved to its permanent home in Indianapolis, Indiana. Predictions for the 1961 race again had a twin-engine dragster taking the win. The Dragmaster *Two Thing* returned, and Eddie Hill's twin Pontiac-powered dragster was there also. Both cars tied for top speed at 170.45. But, it wasn't to be the year for multiple-engine dragsters. A simple, well-engineered, single-engine dragster would take home the Top Eliminator honors. This dragster was driven by Pete Robinson from

While racing another one of his dragsters, Pete Robinson suffered head injuries in an accident. When he built this car, he added a protective shell within the top of the roll bar. The semicircular shell is padded on the inside and adorned with the Goodyear "winged foot" logo on the outside.
INSET

In 1966, Pete Robinson switched to the Ford Single Over Head Cam 427-cubic inch engine, commonly called the "Cammer." Later that year, Robinson became the first to win a major NHRA event with a Ford-powered dragster. In 1970, when Ford Motor Company scaled back its support for the Cammer engine, Robinson continued to run his. He had invested a lot of his time and money into developing special Cammer engine components exclusively for dragsters.

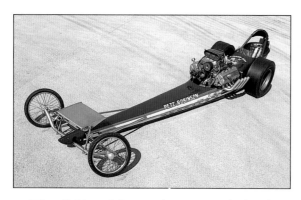

Pete Robinson's first two dragsters were built with a Dragmaster chassis and carried the name *South Wind* and *South Wind #2*. In 1964, he switched to a Woody Gilmore chassis and started the *Tinker Toy* series. It was in a car very similar to this one that Robinson was killed.

Atlanta, Georgia. At 1,280 pounds, Robinson's entry was half the weight of the twin-engine entries. It was powered by a 352-cubic inch supercharged Chevrolet engine.

Robinson was formally trained in engineering at Georgia Tech. Revered by Don Garlits as the best engineer in drag racing, Robinson was always conscious of weight and did everything he could to minimize the weight of his cars. He was once quoted as saying, "Your engine has a certain amount of available power and the less weight it has to propel, the faster and quicker the vehicle will accelerate." Robinson's cars were always well engineered and fast. His inventiveness and engineering prowess earned him the nickname "Sneaky Pete," because he was always one jump ahead of his competitors.

In 1963, Robinson showed up at the U.S. Nationals with jacks that lifted his dragster's rear wheels off the ground. At the starting line, he would raise the car up on the jacks, then engage the clutch to get the rear wheels spinning. When the green light came on, Robinson would drop the jacks and the car would take off like a shot. The NHRA eventually banned the use of jacks, but other sanctioning bodies approved of their use.

Early on, Robinson shied away from the large Chrysler Hemis that were so popular in the dragster classes. He preferred lighter engines like the small-block Chevy. In 1966, Robinson switched to a larger engine—the Ford Single Over Head Cam 427-cubic inch engine, commonly called the "Cammer." It wasn't until late in the year at the Tulsa, Oklahoma, NHRA Points Final, that Robinson became the first to win a major NHRA event with a Ford-powered dragster. Consistency and lightening-fast starts were the keys to Robinson's success. That win also sealed the 1966 NHRA Points Championship for him in the Top Fuel category.

At the 1967 Springnationals held in Bristol, Tennessee, Robinson, with his Ford Cammer-powered dragster *Tinker Toy III*, was low qualifier with an elapsed time of 7.11 seconds. At the time, there were only five Cammer-powered rails in the country. They were all at Bristol and only one failed to qualify. In the Top Fuel final round, Robinson was defeated by the Ford Cammer-powered Baney-Prudhomme car. Prudhomme had qualified fourth and with each successive round, had gotten faster. In the final against Robinson, Prudhomme turned an impressive 6.92 seconds at 220.58 miles per hour.

Robinson's inventiveness caused quite a stir at the 1967 Springnationals. It was there that he debuted his air-driven engine starter. Up until then, dragsters had been started by receiving a stout push down the track from a car or truck. Once up to speed (40 to 50 miles per hour), the clutch would be released and the ignition turned on. This was an unreliable and often dangerous way to start this class of car. Robinson's invention was a modified truck starter spun by an air turbine. Attached to it was an air valve and a length of hose that led to a small tank carrying a supply of air pressurized at 150 psi. The starter attached to the snout of the blower and drove the blower's pulley. When the valve was depressed, it would spin the big Ford engine at 1,400 rpm. Robinson's starter

Pete Robinson's dragsters were always beautifully constructed. He applied his engineering knowledge to make his cars as simple and as light as possible. Tom Hanna built the sleek aluminum body on this dragster.

The big Ford engine's zoomie headers point directly at the rear tires. When first fitted to dragsters, this header design was credited with an increase in performance. Two prominent theories for this additional power have been debated over the years. Some believe the rush of exhaust gasses blows the excessive loose rubber off the spinning slicks, giving them better bite; while others feel that the down force generated by the upward exhausting of gasses forces the rear of the car down on the track, creating better adhesion.

also allowed test firings in the pits, an otherwise impossible task with a push-started dragster.

In 1970, Ford scaled back all of their racing efforts, and their support for the big Cammer engine ended. While most other competitors switched to the Chrysler Hemi, Robinson stayed with the big Ford engine because he'd spent so much of his own time and money developing many of the dragster-specific Cammer components, like the blower drive.

Robinson was also fascinated by ground effects. He theorized that in order to get extra traction, the car's tires needed to "think" the car weighed 1,000

pounds more than it actually did. Early in 1971, when Robinson appeared at Lions Drag Strip, he had a strange-looking rubber spoiler under his dragster, which he claimed was worth 0.20 of a second. Robinson felt this ground-effects device was the answer to obtaining the additional traction he desired. At that meet, he qualified with a low elapsed time of 6.50. Three weeks later at the 1971 NHRA Winternationals, when Robinson staged for his first qualifying attempt, the strange-looking spoiler was under his car. Just after clearing the lights in 6.77 seconds, Robinson's car veered into the right guardrail and disintegrated. Robinson, 37, had survived two other crashes, but this one took his life. A few weeks later, Paul Prichette died in another dragster accident in Arizona. They would be the last front-engine dragster drivers to die. By the end of 1971, all major competitors would be driving rear-engine dragsters.

15

DON PRUDHOMME'S ARMY FUNNY CAR

Don Prudhomme is one of a handful of drag racers who can legitimately be called a legend. He got his start in drag racing by being the best driver of a race car owned by the Road Kings Car Club. In 1962, Prudhomme was vaulted into the Top Fuel spotlight by winning the Smoker's Fuel & Gas meet at Bakersfield, California. There he drove a Kent Fuller chassis, which was powered by a Chrysler Hemi built by Dave Zeuchel. The Smoker's meet was Prudhomme's first big win and

Drag chutes had become standard equipment on drag racing cars in the 1970s. The one on Prudhomme's Challenger Funny Car is mounted high up on the body, just below the spoiler. The fiberglass body is not strong enough to take the resistive forces of the drag chute when it's deployed. The chute needed a major structural component to tug against. On Prudhomme's car, that component is the differential.

INSET

With the body open, the big blown Hemi engine and driver's compartment are exposed. The aluminum panel attached to the body is the firewall; it's intended to separate the driver from any fire as a result of an engine explosion. On that firewall are two small square windows that allow the driver to see what is happening up front. Two fire bottles can be seen, one below the frame rail and one inside the body. The Tony Nancy-stitched seat is surrounded by a very sturdy wraparound roll bar.

Funny Cars have also been called "floppers," because of the way the body opens. Hinged in the rear, a latch in the front releases to swing the body up. With the body in the raised position, the driver climbs into his seat and then the body is lowered. It's impossible for the driver to raise the body while he's in the car. His only escape route is through one of the open side windows.

brought him into national prominence in the drag racing world. The next two legendary dragsters that Prudhomme drove, the Greer-Black-Prudhomme dragster and Roland Leong's *Hawaiian*, confirmed to the world he was one of the best in the sport. Prudhomme loved dragsters and continued his winning ways through the early 1970s.

At that time, Funny Cars were becoming increasingly popular. Funny Cars had grown out of the early Fuel Coupes and the factory A/FX cars. The name Funny Car was probably derived from the unconventional appearance of the altered wheelbase factory experimental cars of the mid-1960s. Soon, a few of these altered wheelbase A/FX cars were sporting superchargers. The die was cast when veteran racer Don Nicholson built what could be considered the prototypical Funny Car. It was based on a tube frame similar to a dragster. The body was a fiberglass replica of a 1966 Mercury Cyclone. It was hinged at the rear, allowing the front of the body to tilt upward. On the strip, it appeared to be a regular passenger car with standard proportions. This offered the Detroit manufacturers strong vehicle identification to a car available to the general public. Passenger car bodies also offered a large area on which to paint sponsor names.

While not quite as fast as Top Fuel dragsters, the Funny Cars put on a spectacular show for the fans, especially at night. The Funny Cars ran nitro, so they had the sound and fire of the Top Fuel dragsters. The Funny Cars' short wheelbase made for some spectacular seemingly out-of-control runs down the quarter. Funny Cars were also able to build rivalries based on their body styles. Once again the fans could enjoy Ford-versus-Chevy-versus-Mopar battles, even though almost all of the Funny Cars were running Chrysler Hemi engines. Showmanship was also part of the Funny Car extravaganza, including long smoky burnouts. Once the tire smoke cleared, they would rump-rump-rump back to the starting line,

often with the aid of a scantily clad female. It was pure vaudeville with a large dose of good old American speed.

While Funny Cars were gaining in popularity, Prudhomme continued driving and winning in Top Fuel cars. In both 1969 and 1970, he won the U.S. Nationals driving a dragster and had no plans to change rides. "I was a real dyed-in-the-wool dragster guy," says Prudhomme. "What happened is that McEwen and I started to do a lot of match racing. I already had the nickname 'the Snake,' and he was 'the Mongoose.' " McEwen, who liked to keep up with the trends, also had a Funny Car that he used to match race with. "One day McEwen came to me and said, 'I know somebody at Mattel Toy Company to see about a sponsorship.' Well, lo and behold, they wanted to do business with us," exclaims Prudhomme, "but they wanted us in Funny Cars." Mattel had done their market research on drag racing and on the popularity of Funny Cars. They felt the Funny Cars would tie in well with their line of Hot Wheels die-cast cars. "We certainly needed the money and that's how it started," says Prudhomme.

"Going into them, I really didn't even like Funny Cars," admits Prudhomme. "They weren't as fast as a dragster, and they had automatic transmissions. When they'd blow up, the automatic transmission fluid would pour out—it was just a mess."

For a while, Prudhomme ran both the dragster and Funny Car. For the 1973 season, John Buttera built Prudhomme a Barracuda-bodied car that he fell in love with. "That car was just unbelievable," exclaims Prudhomme. "It had this bitchin' wraparound roll cage and a trick front end on it, and it was fast—so man, I liked the car. From then on, I forgot completely about dragsters and just stayed focused on Funny Cars." The Barracuda Funny Car that Buttera built for Prudhomme in 1973 was painted bright yellow and carried the Carefree Gum sponsorship along with Hot Wheels. This same car would carry the U.S. Army colors in 1974.

Driving a Funny Car is very different from driving a dragster. The dragster's long wheelbase requires an easy touch on the wheel, whereas the Funny Car begs to be driven. "A dragster is basically easier to drive as long as you don't overdrive it," says Prudhomme. "You have to manhandle a Funny Car. You'd get over by the guardrail and you'd give 'em a little English. You know, you'd kind of whip the wheel to pull it over in the center of the course and you could kinda' get her sideways damn near goin' through the lights. They were, and probably still are, more fun to drive than a dragster. It was fun to do—it was really cool to drive one—it's as simple as that."

Prudhomme excelled behind the wheel of his Funny Cars. In 1973, driving the *Carefree* Barracuda, he became the first driver to win the U.S. Nationals in two different professional classes. In 1966, 1969, and 1970, he took home the title in Top Fuel. Prudhomme kicked off the 1973 Nationals by qualifying with a record-setting time of 6.35 seconds. In the final, he was matched against veteran Funny Car driver Ed "the Ace" McCulloch, who was looking for his third straight Indy win. Prudhomme took the win with an elapsed time of 6.38 seconds and a speed of 229.69 miles per hour.

At the end of the 1973 season, Prudhomme parked the Barracuda and climbed into a new Butterabuilt Vega Funny Car. "It had all kind of widgets and scoops in the front end and louvered rear windows to let the air out." The problem with the new car was that it was severely overweight. "We weren't really that hep to weight back then," says Prudhomme. He tested the new car at Beeline Drag Strip in Phoenix, Arizona. With the engine from the Barracuda, the new Vega was one-tenth of a second slower than the Barracuda. "I thought—wow—what's wrong with this car? We ended up running OK, but I had to beat the engine up to do it." When Prudhomme got back to the shop and checked the weight, he found out the extent of the problem. "The body was way heavier than the Barracuda. The chassis was heavier—everything was

heavier," recalls Prudhomme. "I immediately pulled the engine out of the Vega and sold the car. I took the Barracuda out of storage and did a real number on it to lighten it up. It ended up being a better car than it was the year before. From then on, the rest is history—the car ran really well!"

Prudhomme, now flying the Army colors on his revamped Barracuda, repeated his Nationals

win at Indy in 1974. This time it was young Billy Meyer who challenged Prudhomme for the top honors. Meyer was top qualifier with a 6.28-second elapsed time, and Prudhomme qualified second at 6.29 seconds. In the final against Meyer, Prudhomme ran a solid 6.33 to outdistance the teenager. And as "the Snake" said, the rest is history!

In 1974, Don "the Snake" Prudhomme ran this Dodge Challenger-based Funny Car with the sponsorship of the U.S. Army. When he ran this car in 1973, it was painted yellow and was sponsored by Carefree Gum.

CHAPTER 16

DON GARLITS' *SWAMP RAT 22*

In the early 1970s, Don Garlits had a series of rear-engine dragsters, some more successful than others. One of the most famous of Garlits' rear-engine cars is *Swamp Rat 22*. It was the first dragster to go 250 miles per hour in the quarter-mile, a feat other dragsters were unable to accomplish for seven years. In addition to the speed record, Garlits won both the IHRA (International Hot Rod Association) world title and the NHRA's World Championship in 1975 while driving the *Swamp Rat 22*.

Swamp Rat 22 debuted in the middle of the 1975 race season, replacing *Swamp Rat 21*.

If you look closely, you'll notice that on each side of the cockpit of *Swamp Rat 22*, Garlits has positioned a pair of sideview mirrors. No, they weren't there to watch his competitors disappear behind him. Garlits installed them as a safety measure. When backing up following a burnout, Garlits could see what was going on behind him.

INSET

"Big Daddy" Don Garlits leans against the rear wing of his famous *Swamp Rat 22*. Driving this dragster at the 1975 NHRA World Finals in Ontario, California, Garlits set the NHRA speed record for Top Fuel dragsters at 250.69 miles per hour, a record that stood for seven years.

GARLITS' EPIPHANY

On March 8, 1970, while sitting in his dragster on the starting line at Lions Drag Strip, Don Garlits was the victim of a terrible transmission explosion. This explosion was so horrible, it cut his *Wynn's Charger* dragster in two. Garlits was severely injured, losing part of his right foot. During his six-week recuperation, Garlits formulated his plan to never again sit behind the engine of a Top Fuel dragster. He was going to build a rear-engine dragster—and make it work.

Over the years, there had been a few rear-engine dragsters. None had ever competed successfully in the Top Fuel class. High-speed directional stability had always been the problem. Garlits asked his old friend Connie Swingle to help him with the construction of his new rear-engine car. Swingle was an accomplished dragster driver and, according to Garlits, he was the best chassis welder and fabricator in the business. Garlits credits Swingle for finding the secret to making the rear-engine car work. Swingle slowed down the steering ratio. This took the sensitivity out of the steering and allowed the car to handle properly at high speeds.

Garlits' first rear-engine car, *Swamp Rat 14*, was greeted by laughter when it debuted. In typical Garlits style, he was the one laughing by the time he left the strip. *Swamp Rat 14* kicked off the 1971 racing season by taking Top Eliminator at the NHRA Winternationals, and Garlits never looked back. Don Garlits forever changed the face of drag racing with his rear-engined *Swamp Rat 14*. Within two years, all the top drivers had switched to rear-engine cars.

Garlits' new dragster had a 250-inch wheelbase and was 80 pounds lighter than its predecessor. Powering it was a 480-cubic inch Hemi engine with an estimated horsepower of 2,500. It, like almost all of Garlits' cars, was painted black.

Throughout 1975, Garlits and Top Fuel competitor Gary Beck were in a struggle for the points lead in both the IHRA and NHRA season titles. Beck would win a race, then Garlits would win a race. This duel went on all year long, keeping them within a few hundred points of each other for the championships. At the IHRA season final in Bristol, Tennessee, Beck was a no-show, defaulting the IHRA title to Garlits. Instead of attending the IHRA race, Beck showed up at the NHRA race in Seattle, which was on the same weekend. Garlits, true to his contract with the IHRA, ran the IHRA race, knowing Beck would be gaining valuable points on him in the NHRA's title chase. This set the stage for one of the most exciting events in drag racing history.

The showdown for the NHRA title was at the final race of the season, the Supernationals in Ontario, California. Garlits had a chance, even though he came to the event 400 points behind Beck. During the first day of qualifying, Beck set the e.t. record and Garlits qualified second. Garlits needed the additional points for setting the record and had to outlast Beck in the eliminations.

Garlits had been planning to set the speed record all year long. In his trailer, he had an engine stashed away that was the most powerful he had ever built. He also had squirreled away a pair of slicks that, at 36 inches, were larger in diameter than any others. The larger-diameter tires would produce the

Swamp Rat 22 is powered by a 480-cubic inch Hemi engine with an estimated horsepower of 2,500. Although very similar in design to the early Chrysler Hemis, this engine is all-aluminum and designed just for drag racing.

same effect as changing to a higher gear ratio and Garlits' hot engine would provide the power to turn those tires.

Following qualifying on Friday night, Garlits returned to his motel. (In 1975, the competitors didn't have the big rig haulers for their cars like they do today. The dragsters were towed in a trailer and taken to and from the track each day.) "We went back to this fleabag motel in Montclair, California," says Garlits. "We strung extension lights out of the room and worked all night. We pulled the 250-mile-per-hour engine that I'd been saving out of the rack. We put the engine in and put the tires on the car, and we were ready to go back to the track on Saturday. I told my wife, 'The stage is set for the most dramatic event in drag racing history.'"

When Garlits returned to the track on Saturday, he and the other competitors were greeted by a downpour. Late in the afternoon, the weather started to clear, and Garlits was the first of the Top Fuel competitors to get his car ready. "I strung up a little tarpaulin and got my car out of the trailer," says Garlits. "Everybody was still in their trailer; I was the only one out. We started the engine under the tarp and warmed it up. Everybody came over and asked what I was doin'. I said, 'See that sky, it's going to be clear in a little while, and they're going to make some runs this afternoon—I'm getting ready.' Within 15 minutes you could hear fuel motors cackling throughout the whole place." The sun came out, allowing the track to dry enough to allow cars to qualify. Garlits got in line to run. "Back then you flipped for lane choice, winner gets his choice of lane. I lost the toss for the lane," says Garlits. "My competitor said, 'Big Daddy, I'm tryin' to qualify at this race. I'm sorry I've got to have the good right lane, you're going to have to take the bad left lane.'" Garlits was disappointed because he knew the time was right to make the big run, and he wanted the best possible surface to run on.

Garlits made a rather long burnout to warm the slicks. When he stopped and looked down at the track, he couldn't believe his eyes. His lane was white with rice ash used to absorb oil from a previous competitor's engine that had blown up. When Garlits looked over in the other lane, his competitor wasn't there. When he got back to the starting line, one of his crew members signaled to him that the other guy cut his engine off and wasn't going to make a qualifying attempt. Garlits signaled to the starter, Buster Couch, that he wanted to switch to the now-vacant good right lane, but Couch refused to let him switch.

"I didn't want to do it," Garlits confides. "This was a killer engine that was shakin' the ground. I didn't want to go out there and spin the tires and blow it up. But a voice in the back of my head said, 'Big, make the run.' I pulled up there and I just kinda stepped down on it. The front end came up about a foot off the ground and the front wheels never turned—they just stayed stationary in the air. I wanted to get through this rice ash before I shifted into high, because of the torque when you change gears. I just ran it out in low gear as far as it would go—it was just screamin'. It still hadn't touched the front wheels down yet and it's still goin' straight. They musta put a lot of glue on the track. Even though it was white, it was still sticky. Finally, in high gear, it set the front wheels down and two big whiffs of smoke come off of 'em 'cause it was already running 225 miles an hour. It went through 250.69 miles per hour and 5.63 seconds. We got the record—It was the first car over 250."

The weekend's excitement wasn't over. Garlits wanted to win the NHRA title, but Beck was still leading in points. The extra points given to Beck for setting the e.t. record were effectively canceled out by the points given to Garlits for his record speed run. Unless Beck was eliminated early, Garlits had to set the e.t. record and win the race to clinch the NHRA title. "We won the first round

<D>on Garlits drove *Swamp Rat 22* to both the NHRA and IHRA Top Fuel Championships in 1975. At the end of the year, he put it away and built a new car. In 1977, Garlits pulled *Swamp Rat 22* out of retirement to successfully compete in several match races and in both IHRA and NHRA events.

rather handily," says Garlits. "Then we came up against the *Kentucky Moonshiner* team—that's Robert Frakes and Dale Funk."

"The driver, Dale Funk, came over to flip for lane choice. He told me, 'You just take any lane you want, Big.' On top of that he says, 'Do you want us to red light, fail to fire on the rollers, what do you want us to do? Tell me, and I'll do it!' I looked old Dale right in the eye and I said, 'Dale you know I've been accused of that in the match races. But, you know, I've never laid down on a race and wouldn't ask anybody to lay down on a race. Just go up there and race

and whatever happens—happens.' This great big guy with tears runnin' down his face put his arms around me and says, 'Big Daddy, this is why you're my hero!' Dale then turned to Robert Frakes and yelled, 'Robert, put the nitro in that SOB—the old man wants to race.' They loaded up and ran the best run of their life at 5.80. We ran 5.65."

Garlits' 5.65 elapsed time backed up his e.t. record and now he was pretty even with Beck in the points. In the next round, which was the semifinals, Herb Peterson outran Gary Beck, and it was all over. Garlits was the 1975 NHRA World Champion.

INDEX